MW00572305

I Give

You

My Heart

by
Christina Stark

Claymore Publishing Corporation
Canton, Ohio

Copyright © 1995 by Christina Stark.
All rights reserved.

Claymore Publishing Corporation
2221 Ninth Street, SW
Canton, Ohio 44706

ISBN 1-886681-03-1

Claymore Publishing Corporation offers special discounts for bulk purchases of its products to be used for fund-raising, premium gifts, sales promotions, educational use, etc. Book excerpts or special editions can be produced to specification. For information contact the Special Sales Department at the above address.

Drawings and cover design by
Cheri Miller, P.O. Box 82, East Sparta, Ohio 44626.

Printed in the United States of America.

Dedication

This book is dedicated to my parents, Marion and Joe Brown, who are now deceased. The inspiration for some of the writing was due to circumstances prior to and after their deaths.

They taught me about Jesus and His love, as a little girl, and they are the reason I still serve him today.

I could feel their presence as I wrote the pages of this book.

May you, as the reader, feel that same presence and be richly blessed.

Christina, Dad, Mom, Rose, Gloria

Contents

Contents (con't)

Contents (con't)

Foreword

There could not be a more suitable title for this book, than *I Give You My Heart*. Throughout its pages Christina does give you her heart, all the while capturing the heart of you, the reader.

Her close relationship with the Lord gives her the ability to share with you many of the precious moments in her life. Her poems and stories dispense feelings with simplicity of words and sincerity of expression. Only Christina could compose them in such humorous and yet heart moving fashion.

As you read through the pages, you will be sharing in her joys and sorrows, laughter and tears. I know you will relate to many of the poems and stories, just as I have.

I recommend this book for the reading pleasure of young and old, men and women, the commoner and the famous. If you have not had the privilege of knowing Christina personally, you will feel as if you do after reading this book.

Heart is Christina and Christina is heart!

Pastor Don Bartow

Acknowledgments

To write this book required the talents of my dear friend and neighbor, Cheri Miller. Her faithfulness and talents deserve recognition. You may find it challenging to search for her signature in each drawing.

I'm indebted to my husband Dean, who has been my moral support. He has allowed me to just be myself and never complained over my long hours of typing and late meals. He sat patiently and listened as I read these pages over and over to him. Thanks, Dean. I love you!

I want to thank my daughter Angie, for her encouragement and her persistence in telling me, "Mom, you need to get your book done!"

A special thanks goes to a dear friend, Pastor Bill Bush. He told me to always remember that I am lovable, valuable and capable and that I can do all things through Christ.

I'm grateful to my family and friends for all their prayers and encouragement.

A special recognition goes to Dawn Castel for my makeup and hair design. Also to Jennifer Avers for the photograph.

I'm thankful for my boss Elsie Cowles. My job has allowed me the freedom to fulfill my dreams and still help support my family.

I'm eternally grateful to God for the path He has given me in this life and those He has chosen to cross that path. Without Him, this book would only be a dream. Because of Him, it is now a reality!

Introduction

Well, its been a long time since 1978 and my first publication, *Daisies and Me*. So much has happened during the past seventeen years.

Life can be an interesting and unpredictable journey. I'm inviting you to come along with me.

It's my desire that as you read and then close the final page, that you will know without a shadow of a doubt, that God is a *personal* God.

I Give You My Heart

I Give You My Heart

Life was given to me as a gift
Now some forty years ago
In this time I have often learned
That you reap just what you sow.

With age my wrappings have wrinkled
There are days I get shattered and torn
And it seems I've been untying ribbons
Since the very first day I was born.

There are days I would like to exchange myself
For a package of different design
But a still small voice reminds me
I'm an original and one of a kind.

I wanted to share this gift I've been given
And I asked God just where to start
He said I should take a pen in my hand
And write you the pages of my heart.

Search me, O God, and know my heart;
test my thoughts. Point out anything
you find in me that makes you sad,
and lead me along the path
of everlasting life.

Psalms 139 vs. 23-24, Living Bible

On The Job

They say I am a dispatcher
I send trucks out on the road
The drivers call and ask the rate
And the weight and time to load.
They stop and get their paperwork
And they travel night and day
The separation from their families
Is a price they have to pay.
Long hours on the highway
Fighting scales and DOTs
Waiting lines and hot loads
Bridge tolls and turnpike fees.
I've sent some in wrong directions
Told them north instead of south
They say a lot of confusing things
Come from dispatcher's mouths.
Some are like a brother
Some are like a dad
A day in the life of dispatch
Is like none you've ever had!
I remember a man named Gordy
With a smile upon his face
He was killed and left five children
Who will miss his warm embrace.
If God gives jobs in heaven
I don't even have to guess
I just know there'll be a telephone
And a trip lease on my desk.

He makes a way . . . .

He Makes A Way

Life's waters at times reach high levels
They are muddy and the current gets rough
Will we try to swim or fear sinking?
So often the decision is tough.

God built us a bridge to cross over
All the problems that come our way
It's constructed by Love and Compassion
There's no toll-gate where we have to pay.

We must trust and have faith in the Builder
Who with such precision and grace
Made a way for us to conquer
Any trial that we have to face.

He can calm the troubled waters
Make the winds and storms obey
Through life's trials and temptations
He always makes a way.

Show me Your ways, O Lord;
Teach me Your paths.

Psalm 25-4 KJV

Valleys
to
Victory

Valleys To Victory

It's so nice to be on the mountain
With everything going our way
What a joy to see the sunshine
Come through on a cloudy day.

It's great to be loved by people
And have everyone like what you do
It's wise to set goals and visions
And rejoice as you see them come true.

There are times while we are climbing
We so easily stumble and fall
And we end up in the valley
Broken and scarred by it all.

I have found that my times in the valley
Were the greatest blessings to me
For when I was down, I had to look up
To the One who would take care of me.

My valley may not be your valley
Your mountains could be higher than mine
But God will give us the victory
If we are only willing to climb.

Thanks be to God, which giveth us
the victory through our Lord Jesus Christ.

1st Corin. 15-57 (KJV)

He didn't see the cross He saw the crown

He Didn't See The Cross, He Saw The Crown

When Jesus learned of His Father's plan
That He would die for every man
He didn't see the cross
He saw the crown.

When Jesus' back was ripped and in pain
He knew it all was not in vain
He didn't see the cross
He saw the crown.

When Jesus felt the thorns upon His head
And blood ran down in crimson red
He didn't see the cross
He saw the crown.

When Jesus' hands and feet were nailed
He knew that Satan's plan had failed
He didn't see the cross
He saw the crown.

When Jesus was pierced deep in His side
Hanging all alone and crucified
He didn't see the cross
He saw the crown.

When Jesus walked out of the grave
All sinners lost could now be saved
He didn't see the cross
He saw the crown.

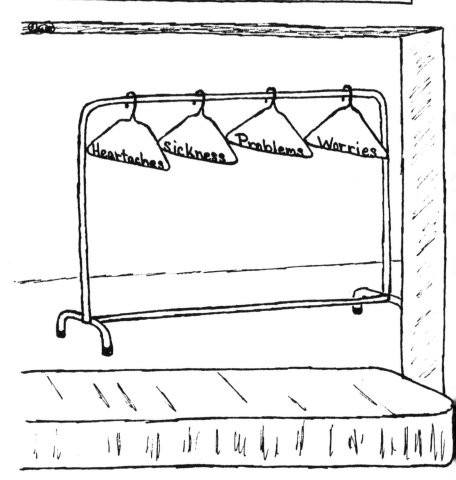

Checking In

Have you ever gone out to dinner
Checked your coat in at the door
And after paying at the counter
You got your coat and tipped once more?

Well, listen very closely
Here's a lesson to be learned
I'll tell you about a check-in gate
Where nothing is returned.

The same man is on duty
Twenty-four hours of the day
You can leave him all your problems
And you never have to pay.

He's in the Burden Business
Drop your heartaches at the door
Remember once you check them in
They're not yours anymore.

Make this a daily habit.
It's worthwhile and it's free
The only requirements are faith and trust
For His Check-In Policy.

Weeding the Seeds You've Sown

Weeding The Seeds You've Sown

There's a purpose for planting seeds, you know
Far more than just so things can grow
The Bible says that if you have a need
The thing to do is plant a seed.

Once it's planted the roots spread out
And very soon it begins to sprout
That one little seed multiplies by the score
But now must come the inevitable chore.

The things we plant get surrounded by weeds
In the garden of life we all have many needs
If you're planting love, weeds of hatred may grow
If you planted money, your income may slow.

If you planted food, your cupboards may be bare
If you planted kindness, no one may care
When the weeds of the enemy take over your crop
There is only one way you can get them to stop.

Begin to start hoeing down the rows of your life
Pull out the anger, bitterness and strife
This will allow God's Son to shine through
Producing a bountiful harvest for others and you.

Open

Account

Open Account

You can have IRAs and government bonds
All sorts of ways to invest
But I have found that serving God
Has proved to be the best.

God has an open bank account
The checks are written free
He loans without deposits
And charges no monthly service fee.

There are no drive-up windows
No standing in long lines
The hours are never scheduled
You may request at any time.

His hand is always on the pen
Just let him know your heart's desire
He never asks for references
Trust is all that is required.

Whether rich or poor it's all the same
He doesn't give by what you make
No waiting clause or closing costs
Or a limit on what to take.

At the bank of the Holy Spirit
The customer is number one
It is backed by the greatest investors
Our Heavenly Father and His Son.

Demon's Delight

Demon's Delight

Each night as I lie sleeping
Someone guards my bed
Waiting for me to awaken
To put bad things in my head.

He holds a tray of discontentment
With cups of anger, jealousy and fear
So I must daily put on the armor
That the Lord has standing near.

I need the helmet of salvation
So my mind will stay on track
Carry the shield of faith to protect me
When Satan begins to attack.

I need the breastplate of righteousness
So I can do my very best
Shod my feet with preparation
And stand ready for the test.

I must gird my loins about with truth
And when Satan tells me lies
With the sword of the Spirit
I can sound my battle cry.

I must choose this day whom I will serve
As a soldier I must fight
To resist the things brewed up for me
On the tray of Demon's Delight.

Say One for Me

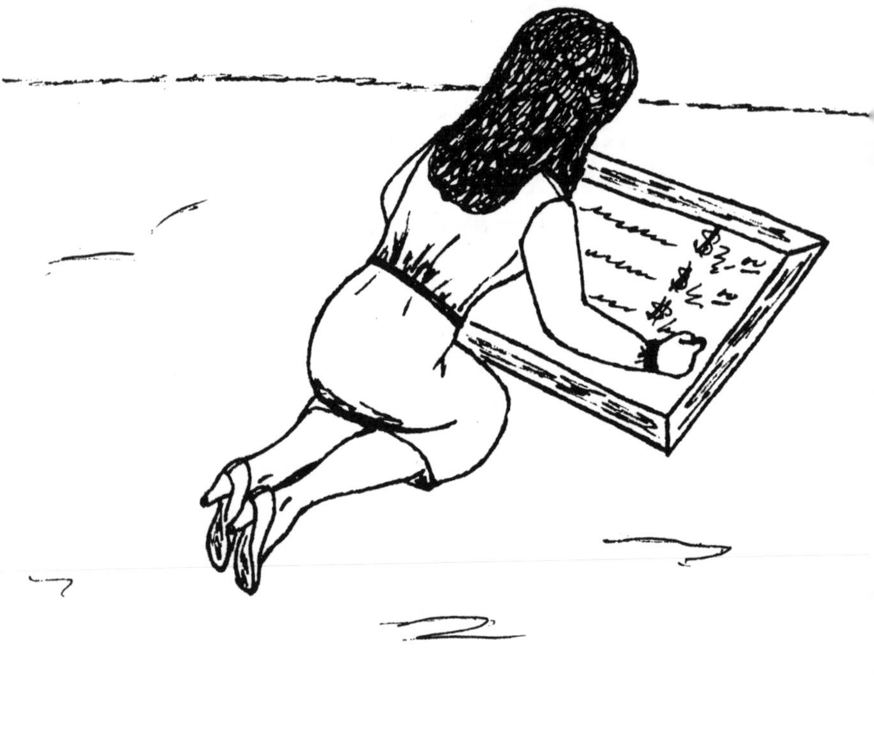

Say One For Me

While working as a hostess
I would daily write the board
It was the strangest way I'd ever had
To share about the Lord.

On my knees I'd write the menus
And the specials of the day
The customers arriving early
Would often stop and say.

"Hey while you're kneeling down there,
Please say one for me."
I'd tell them I'd be happy to
And we would talk about their needs.

Some had loved ones who were sick
While others needed a job
Many were blessed abundantly
But wanted a closer walk with God.

It was good to hear reports come in
Such as, "Mom feels better today."
Or, "I start my new job tomorrow."
"I even got a raise in pay."

Every job can be rewarding
Wherever you may choose to be
Always listen for the person
Who says, "Hey, say one for me!"

Mrs. Gonna

I'm gonna do this and I'm gonna do that
Are words I say every day
Yet nothing gets done, cause I manage to let
Everything get in my way.

I'm gonna go here and I'm gonna go there
Yet I never get on the right track
My intentions are good, but I never get far
It seems like something keeps holding me back.

I'm gonna start now or perhaps even later
Yet I stop before I begin
My bases are loaded and I'm striking out
Before life gets the first pitch in.

I'm gonna say this and I'm gonna say that
But I never say much that makes sense
Though gifted with quite an intelligent mind
I so often act like I'm dense.

I'm gonna be this and gonna be that
But I'm still what I've always been
Just when I think I've discovered myself
Then whoops, I've lost me again!

Yes there are things I've talked of doing
Since I was just a kid
I'd like a message on my tombstone
That reads, "Mrs. Gonna . . . finally did!"

O' Christmas Tree

O' Christmas Tree

Every year the search got underway
For the perfect Christmas tree
I would try so hard to find the one
That would be coming home with me.

I would talk to them and sing them songs
Decorate them in my mind.
How could I ever pick just one
Out of all those different kinds?

I've got my car stuck in the mud
Waded snow up to my knees
Nothing was too hard for me
To bring home that special tree!

I have cut them down and shaped them up
Turned them all around the room
Placed the lights and then the bulbs
While singing all the Christmas tunes.

You can say it's age or wisdom
But I could not resist the price
Now our Christmas tree comes in a box
Which has really been quite nice.

No more falling needles
And no water on the floor
There no longer is a struggle
Coming through the entrance door.

I just go into the attic
Put four pieces all together
I don't have to go out of the house
In all that winter weather.

I still have mixed emotions
But the tree is here to stay
I just get a can of holiday pine
To spray on Christmas day!

Dear Dad

They said it would get easier
As time lingered on
That I wouldn't feel this heartache
So long after you were gone.
But there hasn't been a day go by
When I haven't thought of you
You're still so much a part of
Everything I say and do.
Little things like lima beans
Can bring tears into my eyes
Even a cup of McDonald's coffee
Makes me think of you at times.
There will be no more cards at birthdays
No more candles on your cake
When the 20th of March passed by this year
I thought my heart would break.
When songs come on the radio
That remind me so of you
I often listen for your whistle
And the humming of your tune.
I'd love to hear your laughter
Have you answer the telephone
Walk up the steps to your front porch
And find you still at home.
I'd love to cook your favorite meal
Have you make fun of my biscuits
Bring over something broken
And watch you as you'd fix it.
I'm sorry you missed Angie
As she stood in her wedding gown

Without a doubt, you would have been
The happiest grandfather around.
Holidays are different now
The table has an empty chair
How I'd love to walk into the room
And find you sitting there.
When I go over to the graveyard
To fix the flowers for each season
I thank God that you are with Him
Yet, I'm still searching for a reason.
How could a tiny tumor
Inside someone's brain
Destroy a man as strong as you
And cause you so much pain?
You were a man who lifted bars of steel
Sometimes sixteen hours a day
Near the end you couldn't hold a fork
Or tell us what you had to say.
Before your operation
You accepted Jesus Christ
He became the rock you leaned on
As you struggled to survive.
During a "near death experience"
You told of how you entered in
To a place of wondrous beauty
Where you took a walk with "Him."
He led you through the pastures
Of a paradise so rare
You wanted to take pictures
But He said you'd soon be there.
As I listened so intently
To a story only you could tell
You said, "I'm glad of one thing baby,
Your daddy did not see hell."

I guess that day I realized
Someone else was in control
More important than your healing
Would be the condition of your soul.
Every time I'd hear the phone ring
My heart would pound inside
Would this be the final hour?
Would this be the day you died?
Yes, it was one whole year of ups and downs
But you never lost your smile
You always greeted everyone
In your special "Joe Brown" style.
In dreams I get a glimpse of you
And often see your smiling face.
I can hear your voice call out to me
And feel your warm embrace.
Dad, you left me a great inheritance
Far more than wealth and fame
What a privilege in life I was given
To be your child and bear your name.

In loving memory of my father
William J. Brown
who died April 8th, 1988

Put Me Back Together

Lord, I feel just like a puzzle
That's been thrown into a box
While in life's daily struggles
Many pieces have been lost.

Parts of me are everywhere
Scattered to and fro
Will I ever be the same again
Is all I want to know?

I'm lined up on the outside
The inside pieces just don't fit
I'm tired of all the hassles
Now it's up to you, I quit!

Please put be back together
And this time use some glue
Lord the picture of my puzzle
Is nothing without you.

Borrowed Time

Borrowed Time

Have you ever thought of how it would be
When you left this world for eternity
Would it be at the fate of an automobile
Or some deadly disease that made you so ill?

Would it be on some long awaited vacation
Or perhaps at the peak of a festive occasion
Would it be in an earthquake or even a flood
Maybe someone could shoot you down in cold blood?

Would you suffer at length or go rather fast
Or die broken hearted over things of the past
Would you die leaving wealth or not even a dime?
Do you know that you're living on life's borrowed
time?

> *Whereas ye know not what shall be on the morrow.*
> *For what is your life? It is even a vapor,*
> *that appeareth for a little time*
> *and then vanisheth away.*
>
> **James 4-14 (KJV)**

Quiet Times

Quiet Times

Give me an old log cabin
Nestled way back in the hills
With a worn out bed to sleep in
Under a fluffy patchwork quilt.
Give me a rustic window sill.
Where I can perch my coffee cup
And look out through the window pane
And watch the sun come up.
Give me a rocker on an old front porch
Where I can waste away the hours
Viewing nature's masterpiece
Of blooming wildwood flowers.
Give me an old pot belly stove
And some simmering potpourri
A kerosene lamp giving off a glow
And a favorite book to read.
Give me a toasty campfire
On a chilly autumn night
So I can gaze into the stars
While the moon is shining bright.
Give me a squirrel on a split-rail fence
Eating a nut that fell from a tree
Let me watch the blue jays
Fly around so gleefully.
Give me a little "quiet time"
We all need it now and then
By stepping back into the past
We can face the present once again.

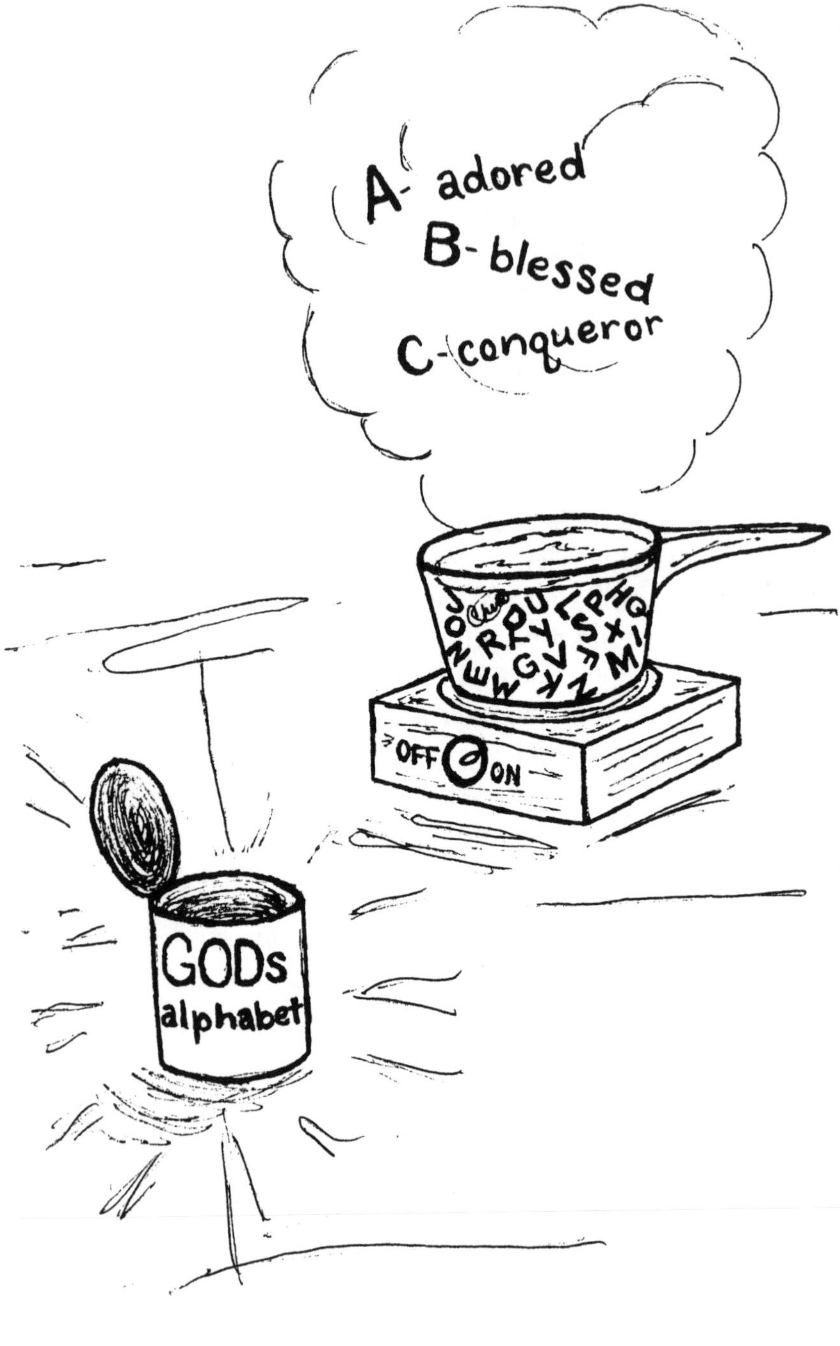
A- adored
B- blessed
C- conquer
OFF ON
GODs
alphabet

God's Alphabet

Campbell was famous for its alphabet soup
I ate it when I was a kid
One day in a study, I learned this for sure
There's a lot more under the lid.
Campbell has nothing over on God
He has a soup on the market today
When you are feeling low and depressed
Read what the letters are trying to say.

A-adored
B-blessed
C-conqueror
D-delivered
E-enriched
F-favored
G-glorified
H-honorable
I-inspired
J-justified
K-kind
L-loveable
M-magnified

N-noble
O-obedient
P-precious
Q-quieted
R-rich
S-secure
T-thankful
U-upright
V-victorious
W-wise
X-xeno (different)
Y-yoked
Z-zealous

You're all the above
And a whole lot more
It's the best selling soup
At God's grocery store.

Friends, Like Sisters

Friends Like Sisters

I have friends I can talk to
For hours on end
Some it will be years
Before I see them again.
I have friends I can dream with
And share all my goals
Those I can pray with
For another one's soul.
I have friends who will tell me
When I've done something wrong
And when I am weak
They prove to be strong.
I have friends who have been there
When a loved one has died
Though their lives were busy
They stood by my side.
I have friends I can laugh with
And with some I can cry
If I offer a challenge
They give it a try.
I have friends I can lean on
When I'm at my wits' end
They will tell me to hold tight
And try once again.
I have friends more like sisters
Who are both young and old
And their value is greater
Than silver and gold.

One Step
at
a
time

One Step At A Time

Life is like a stairway
That seems a long way to the top
The longer you wait to make a move
The easier it is to stop.

The higher you go the harder it gets
But the lessons are worth all the pain
Don't stop in the middle or try to go down
It's like one unbreakable chain.

Use Christ as your rail that you lean on
Take only one step at a time
Soon you will learn you're not in it alone
And it's quite an enjoyable climb.

P A I N

yes

Choices For Pain

Let's face it, life is a battle
We are daily going to war
Suffering comes to God's people
As well as the rich and the poor.

But we have some choices to consider
It's a matter of which will it be
One is for evil and one is for good
Do you really want to be set free?

Some go to drugs and some go to pills
Others try drinking their booze
But if you need a more reliable source
I'll tell you the best thing to choose.

Prayer is the key to whatever you have
Whether terminal or just a bad cold
It's good for a heartache or loss of a friend
But you can't buy it with silver or gold.

You won't pay a doctor, just call on the Lord
It's the best choice that you'll ever make
Whatever the way that your healing may come
It's the safest thing you'll ever take.

Flames Of Freedom

I wonder what Betsy Ross would say
If she were living here today?
Would she believe what people do
To America's flag, red, white and blue?

Once respected and flying high
It's stars and stripes against the sky.
Now it's burned and mocked by scores
And spat upon from shore to shore.

Home of the brave, land of the free
What's happened to our liberty?
Where's the justice for which we stand
Is there still unity in our land?

May the flames of freedom rage within
God forgive this nation for its sin.
Help rid our country of its hate
My only prayer, it's not too late!

Bottled Tears

Bottled Tears

Psalms 56 says God bottles tears
That everyone has cried
Is this a parable or a fact?
I can't figure it out, though I've tried!

How big are the bottles
Are the sizes the same
Does each have a label
That's recorded by name?

Are they mixed with each other's
Or are mine by themselves
Is there a room up in Heaven
Where they sit upon shelves?

Does he blend those of happiness
And those shed in fear
With the millions and millions
We've cried over the years?

Though I don't understand it
Or how it could ever be done
I know nothing is impossible
For God and His Son.

Stumbling block
to
Stepping Stone

Wisdom

Knowledge

Solution

Problems

Stumbling Block To Stepping Stone

Many things may cross our path
We may stumble along the way
But look at them as stepping stones
In our life from day to day.

What may seem to be a problem
Could be a blessing in disguise
A solution to a miracle
Right before our eyes.

Experiences give us knowledge
To deal with all life's ups and downs
Through ignorance we learn wisdom
To fight in these final rounds.

Everywhere our feet go
A lesson will unfold
It begins when we are younger
And carries on as we grow old.

So if you should feel a stumble
Get a grip and try again
You will never know by quitting
How many steps it took to win.

The Feast

The Feast

The Master is sitting with arms open wide
Saying, "Come to my table and eat."
"The banquet is spread, the food is prepared,
Please come and pull up a seat."

If you're feeling sad and lonely
Scoop a little joy off of the plate
If you're all confused and doubtful
Hope and peace will be just great.

If you're mean and unforgiving
Savor a little love and grace
Faith, mercy and wisdom
Add extra spicing to the taste.

You may ask for second helpings
Leaving full is a command
In a hurry? There's a take-home box
The chef will understand.

There's nothing too much trouble
For the Master's honored guests
If in need of reservations
They are made upon request.

My Wish For You

There are those who believe if they toss a penny
Into the bottom of a well
They can close their eyes and make a wish
And things will be just swell.

There are those who think if they wish on a star
Somehow their luck will soon change
Many make wishes as they blow out their candles
Hoping to live to a very old age.

There are those who keep wishing for the day
When all their dreams will come true
To be happy in life and have many blessings
Are the things I am wishing for you.

The Ring

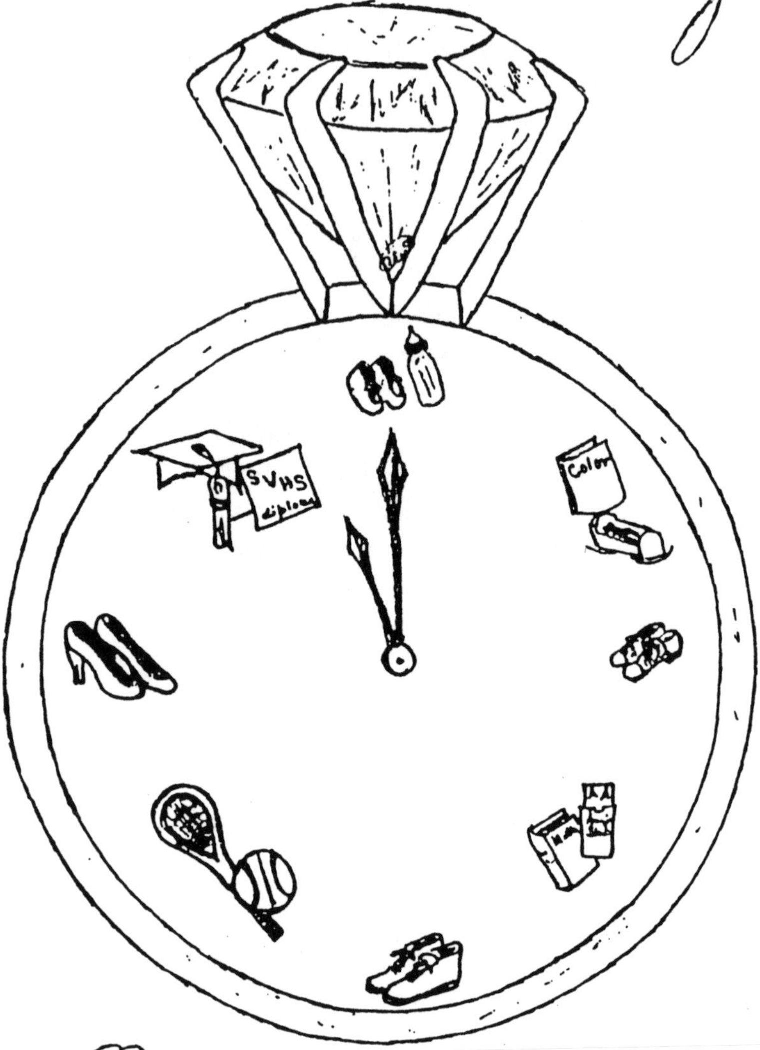

Of Time

The Ring Of Time

Your engagement came as a big surprise
It's like you suddenly grew before our eyes
Yes, since December of 1989
I've traveled throughout the ring of time.

Your baby shoes with lace and bows
That covered up your tiny toes
Were forever bronzed and on display
As we watched you grow from day to day.

Your bottles that I'd warm just right
To help you go to sleep at night
Were soon replaced with drinking cups
With cartoon friends you loved so much.

Your first day of school in brand new shoes
As you rushed off the bus sharing all the news
And I worried all day of how things would go
Then your laughter assured me, it need not be so.

Your fourth grade teacher said you were a whiz in math.
When spelling bees came you were ahead of the class
The years seemed to fly as they so often do
Soon it was high school books and basketball shoes.

Your skills at tennis only lasted a while
But you just had to try it in your very own style
Then came the proms with high heels and fun
We looked at so many dresses to find just the right one.

Your graduation was a gala affair
We laughed and had fun with all who were there
And now look, honey, it's your wedding day
Oh, there's still so much I want to say.

You're all we had, there will be no more
To come bursting through our kitchen door
They say I have to set you free
But you'll always be a part of me.

Your husband will now be number one
And I thank God he'll be our son
Today begins a brand new life
You're still our baby, yet Michael's wife.

God has protected you over the years
He's shared in your laughter, heartache and tears
He'll be listening today as you both say, "I do."
Remember there's never a problem He can't see you
through.

Your father and I now must give you away
And your name will be Farber beginning today
God bless you and keep you in his tender care
And if you ever need us, we will always be there.

Nov. 10th, 1990

I Believe

Like a cloud of darkness covering a full moon, a sudden change came into my life. A storm was raging inside of me. The God I had believed in for so long had deserted me. I was throwing in the towel. It was over.

What about all those verses in the Bible, where by His stripes we are healed? Or, call unto me and I will answer thee and show thee great and mighty things. I called and I called, but to me, He didn't answer. At least, not in the way I wanted Him to.

A dear friend of mine was dying of cancer. Patty had been so excited about having a baby after all those years. During her pregnancy it was discovered she had cancer. After his birth she found out it spread to her liver. Every day I would go to see her, she would say to me, "Oh Chris, you're so lucky, you will live to see Angie grow up, but I won't live to see my son." It was heartbreaking for me and I couldn't even imagine how she must feel. I would go out into the hall and cry and plead with God to save her life. The morphine shots did little to ease her pain, but she always had thanks and praise on her lips. I would tell God she did not deserve this and question what He intended to do.

I got out of bed one night and told my husband I was going up to visit her and pray for her healing. He even knelt by the foot of the bed and prayed with me before I left. She was tossing and moaning when I arrived. I asked her if there was anything she would like to have and she asked for a glass of lemonade. I got the nurse to call down to the cafeteria and send it up. It was brought in a plastic glass with no ice. Anger welled up inside of me. I wanted to go down to that kitchen and say, "This might be the last thing she ever drinks, couldn't it have at least been in a crystal glass with lots of ice and a pretty lemon wedge?" But I remained quiet as I pressed it to her parched lips. Its bitterness made her spit it out and she lay back on the pillow as if to give up.

Unable to keep myself from crying in front of her, I kissed her good-by and went home. I crawled back into bed and while still fully awake, but with my eyes closed, I had what some may call a vision. The Lord was in her room standing beside her bed. He was just looking at her so tenderly. He walked over to her window and looked out for awhile, then came back to her bed again. It was then He stood at her door with His arm leaning against it, as if to look at her one more time and then He walked away. The whole time this was going on, I was explaining to my husband what I was seeing. As He walked out the door, I began to cry hysterically and said, "He's leaving and he's not going to heal her." Two days later she passed away.

There wasn't a dry eye at the funeral services as the pastor read a letter she left behind, telling of her love for God. I left there with a million questions to which there seemed to be no answers.

Days turned into weeks and I was growing farther and farther away from God. Yet there was never a time when I desired to draw closer to Him. Nothing made sense to me anymore. I tried reading the Bible, but I'd get to verses about healing and then close it up in disgust. Was He really there and did He really care?

I needed some answers! A local book store was having their annual sale. I was determined that if I couldn't find the answers in the Bible, then I was going to buy any book I found pertaining to hope. There had to be an answer in one of those. For two days, I sat and read, but found no answers. Being a writer, there were a couple things that got my attention. In two of the books, the authors mentioned that they went to a place called Cape Cod to do their writing. It was there, that they found the peace and relaxation to inspire them. I folded one of those books over my lap and said to my husband, "Cape Cod must be a beautiful place, because two of these authors went there to write their books." He just nodded, but it was then I prayed to God, "How I would love to just get away and find you again, you seem so far away."

I went back to the same store a couple of days later. I had not benefited anything from the previous books. While I was browsing through the store, I ran into a girlfriend of mine. I was very surprised to see her, because she had moved to Massachusetts. I asked her what she was doing here.

With the eyes of an angel, she looked at me and said, "I really don't know why I am here, but God wants me to tell you that He loves you and that you are very special to Him." She also felt I should come out and spend a week with her and her family in Massachusetts. We both began to cry. We had been spiritual friends for too long, not to know that God was about to do something. It was then that I told her I did not have the extra money to take the trip. She said, that her husband told her to tell me that he would pay my air fare home and I could ride back with her.

As we went to leave the store, I saw a calendar with a picture of a lighthouse. I looked at her and said, "Isn't this beautiful?" "I just love lighthouses." She replied that she did too. Then came the words I will never forget. "If you come home with me, I will take you to Cape Cod to see a lighthouse." As the tears flowed down my face, I uttered these words, "If I can sing the song, "The Lighthouse," in the top of a lighthouse, then I'll believe in miracles again." I had been singing that song in our church and I loved the message in it. I also knew that this was a challenge that even God may find difficult.

I invite you on this journey of miracles.

Spending Money

Even though I did not have to pay my way out or back, there were still a few things I needed for the trip. Since this all came so suddenly and I was not working at the time, I just didn't have the funds to splurge on a pair of jeans and some new tennis shoes. Again I went to God. I told him if He wanted me to go on this trip, that I needed a few things before I left. I went to the post office that morning in hopes that I just may get an unexpected insurance check or a refund of some kind. I went from not believing in God, to actually expecting to find some money that He had dropped in there Himself. But I left empty handed and wondered all the way home what I was going to do. I had just opened the door when the phone rang and it was a dear friend of mine. She hadn't seen me in a while and was wondering what I had been doing. I excitedly told her about my trip. She said she was going to be over this way and wanted to know if she could stop in for a few minutes. I was looking forward to her warm smile and friendly conversation. We visited for a while, and as she went to leave, she handed me an envelope and said, "Here is a little something for your trip." Inside I found a $100.00 bill! I went to the store and bought my jeans and tennis shoes and still had some left over. It had been weeks since I felt such happiness. What was going on?

Personal God

Upon arriving at my friend's house, I was resting and reading, yet another book. This one dealt on the matter of whether God was a personal God. I asked her if she believed that. She looked at me and said, "Before this week is over, I think you are going to find out just how personal God really is!"

Chatham Lighthouse

Armed with a cassette and recorder in hand, we headed out for our destination, the Chatham Lighthouse. There it stood touching the sky, as if to say, "Welcome, I am the watchman over this vast ocean." What a comfort it must have been to the many ships directed in by its beacon light. Suddenly, I knew that the ship of life I had been sinking in, was coming to shore.

We entered the guard house to get permission to tour the inside. There we heard the shocking news, that it was being renovated and they were not allowing tourists inside. Jeannie began to explain to the man about all the miles I had traveled to get there. He was not impressed, but a young man volunteered to take us in. God had moved on our behalf!

The only way I can explain it after climbing to the top, was the Biblical passage that says, "the Spirit of God was hovering over the face of the waters." I hardly remember two words that our guide told us. I had one goal in mind and that was to sing! Although finding my request a little strange, he was gracious enough to honor it, and let me sing my lighthouse song. I don't think I have ever sang with such an anointing as I did that day. It was as if all of Heaven's angels were my back up choir. Tears were streaming down my face, as I cried out to God, "I believe, I believe!"

On our way down the stairs, we were able to share our miracle story with the young man. I wanted him to know the song I sang, was about a different lighthouse, and that was Jesus Christ. No one will ever make me believe that he was not supposed to be on duty that day.

A cement base surrounded the lighthouse and it was there, I paused and thanked God for giving me the desire of my heart. As I rose to my feet, there were several men staring out the window. Little did they know, that they had just witnessed a miracle at Chatham Lighthouse.

A Truck, Two Men, And A Rope

We ventured out to see the ocean at Cape Cod. I had been to an ocean before, but this was altogether different. I felt like if I took one step, I would drop off the face of the earth. I wasn't sure if a whale would come and swallow me up, or if Jesus would appear walking on the water.

I wrote Dean a love message in the sand and put some in a little bag to bring home with me. I also gathered a few sea shells, which would later be used as part of my next miracle.

On the way out of the Cape Cod area, we passed a car that seemed to be stuck in the sand. We noticed it was two women, so we decided to turn around and offer our help. They had stopped to have a little picnic on their lunch hour and got their tires buried in the sand. The language one of them was using would have made your hair curl. We introduced ourselves and they joked about us being their two angels. We tried several methods to get their car out, including trying to scoop the sand from under the tire with our sea shells. Nothing we tried was working.

It was then that I told them to get in a circle and I was going to pray for help. I also informed the one who was cussing that I was not going to pray for God to get her out of that mess, if she was going to keep using His name in vain. She happily agreed not to cuss anymore and we all joined hands. You see at this time, my faith was beginning to rise.

I prayed, "Lord you said when we have done all we can do, to stand. Now we have done all we can do. Please send us a truck, two men, and a rope. Amen."

The two women just stood there, but Jeannie and I went out to the road to watch for our help. I laughed as I yelled down to her and told her that I always wanted to direct traffic. It was only a few minutes when she excitedly hollered, "Here comes our truck." Yes, and there were two men in it. They pulled up to the scene and asked if there was anything they could do to help. I told them we had just prayed they would come. They were even a little confused, because they said they weren't even supposed to be on that road. They informed us that all they had in the back of the truck was a rope, but they would be glad to try and get them out. That's all I asked for. A truck, two men, and a rope. While they were getting those two women out of their predicament, we shared the miracle story with them. One of the ladies said that she had been out of church for a long time, but she definitely wanted to get back. Especially after seeing God move on their behalf the way He did that day.

A personal God does things like that!

Boston Commons Park

It was time for a little history and a visit to the park, especially when I heard that the squirrels in this park would eat right out of your hand. I felt like a kid at Christmas when we went and bought peanuts and headed for the park. Word had it, that the park was usually full of squirrels, but that day, we could find none. I stood there with my bag of peanuts looking around for some sign of life and gave a request to God to please send me a squirrel to eat from my hand. Out of nowhere, it came and it was hungry. When it was full, I stood up and looked at Jeannie and said, "Where are the rest of them?" She laughed and said, "You said for God to send you _a_ squirrel." Not only was He personal, He was specific.

King's Chapel

Nestled among the historic buildings near the park, was a beautiful little church, called King's Chapel. It was unlike anything I had ever seen. There were no pews like we have today, but little cubicles where people gathered close together to worship. You could almost sense the presence of families and friends. At the front was an altar. I thought of all the people walking the streets. Everybody in a hurry! Yet there it was; an instrument of peace. I looked at Jeannie and told her that I just had to kneel there and thank God for all that He had done for me so far. We prayed together for a while and were getting ready to leave, when a man approached us. He began to tell us that he couldn't help noticing that we knelt to pray and that he admired our courage to do so. Once again, I had the opportunity to share about everything that had happened and told him there was no way I could leave there without praying. He was a pastor, yet he found it difficult to kneel and pray. He invited us to a very prestigious area that night for a service, but we felt we weren't properly dressed. It's been a decision we have always regretted. We'll always wonder if there was another miracle we missed out on.

The Train Ride

One of my dreams had always been to ride a train. When you live in a small town, a lot of things seem exciting, but nothing could describe that train station in Boston. I don't know which fascinated me more, the height of the ceiling, the sound of the train, or all the people. Once we got the schedule, we knew we had to make a mad rush before departure. We prayed, "Lord please let us make it in time." According to our watch, we should have missed it. Upon arriving, we noticed a girl looking at her watch and prancing back and forth across the platform. We asked her if the train had gone already and she disgustedly told us, that she had ridden that train for years and it had never been late. We looked at each other and smiled. We knew why the train was late! God had done it again! It was so exciting to get to meet a real life conductor and get my ticket punched just like they do on TV. But God had a young girl on that train who needed someone to talk to. She just happened to sit by us. While He was blessing us, He allowed us to be a blessing to her. Was the train late? No, it was right on time!

Betty's Curtains

Jeannie had a neighbor who lived across the street. Betty had a way of making you feel you were one of her best friends. While visiting her and admiring her lovely home, she mentioned that she wanted to get a pair of new curtains to hang at her kitchen window. I asked her what kind she wanted and she said, "I'd love a pair of yellow cape cod curtains with maybe a little orange flower on them." She said they needed to be forty-five inches long. Being a woman and knowing what it's like to want something, I had a desire to buy her those curtains. Not only did I have the desire, but I really felt this was something that God wanted me to do. I didn't have very much money left and I was still looking to find a black and red jogging suit. Could all this be possible with only $20.00? Off to the shopping center we went. I headed straight for the curtain department. All the way through the aisles, I was looking for a pair of yellow curtains and I saw none. I looked several times just in case I might be missing anything. They were not there! I walked away from the curtain department and all the way out I was telling God that I knew He wanted me to buy her those curtains and asked Him why they weren't there. I felt someone saying to me, "Go look again." I argued with the inner voice that I had just looked all over that department and they were not there.

Again came the voice, "Go look again." I walked back through the aisles, feeling it was just a waste of time. Something said, "Look down." As I did, there was a plastic bag with a pair of yellow cape cod curtains with little orange flowers. They were, of course, forty-five inches long. What was even more difficult to believe, was the price. One dollar and fifty cents! I ran to the department that Jeannie was in and showed her the curtains. I said, "There must be a mistake in this price, I'm going to see a sales clerk." The clerk assured me that was the right price. They were a discontinued item that had been marked down and all the pieces were there, including the tie backs. I told her it was a miracle and shared a little with her about Betty's desire to have those curtains.

I also got my heart's desire for that jogging suit. It was so beautiful. It just so happened that I hit the blue light special and got two pair of pants to go with it. All for twelve dollars!

How do you buy a jogging suit with two pair of pants and a pair of cape cod curtains for under twenty dollars? The secret it to take God shopping with you. He is the best bargain hunter in the world!

Well, Betty got her curtains and she was so blessed by hearing the story of how I found them. She needed uplifted and encouraged in her walk with God. After we shared all of the miracles that had taken place that week, she witnessed the reality of a personal God.

The Finale

If any of you have ever traveled in downtown Boston, and you're still alive to talk about it, that is a miracle! We were on our way to the airport and running late. They were announcing the call for the final passengers to board just as we got there. As a little girl, I used to watch movies of how people would have to run to catch their planes and that always seemed so exciting to me. Well, I literally had to run to get on that plane. I turned around to Jeannie and yelled, "I always wanted to run to catch a plane." God was there in the beginning and he was there until the end. Yes, I believe in miracles!

WIT
&
WISDOM

Perfect Conditions

Have you ever planned for a picnic
And had it pour the rain
Set the date for a special meeting
And have everyone complain?

Have you ever cooked a hearty meal
To find that everyone had eaten
Played a game your very best
Yet still got badly beaten?

Have you ever bought an outfit
That you simply just adored
And see the person sitting next to you
Had shopped at the same store?

Have you ever rushed back to the house
Parked your car for just a minute
Closed the door and realized
Your keys were still left in it?

Have you stood in line for groceries
And were "short" to pay the bill
While choosing what you could afford to keep
You were given looks to kill?

Have you ever done the laundry
Opened the lid to your surprise
And found the whites had turned to colors
Right before your eyes?

Have you ever gone for a Sunday drive
And tried to find your way around
You were heading north, but ended up south
In some deserted part of town?

Have you ever gotten up early
With a list of things to do
And felt lucky to accomplish one
Before the day was through?

Have you waited for perfect conditions?
They may never come your way
So just try to make the best of life
Each and every day.

*If you wait for perfect conditions,
you will never get anything done.*

Ecclesiastes 11-4 (Living Bible)

Second Chances

Have you wanted to say, "I love you."
To a family member or friend
Do you have a card still on your desk
You never took the time to send?

Have you thought of paying a visit
To a neighbor down the street
Or perhaps someone moved into town
You never took the time to meet.

Have you wanted to say you're sorry
For a wrong you may have done
Or missed a golden opportunity
To talk to your daughter or your son?

Did you want to thank someone special
But put it off another day
To find the one who blessed you so
Had suddenly slipped away?

I wish I could have back all the chances
I have missed throughout my life
When I could have done a whole lot more
As a mother, friend and wife.

I would have been a little kinder
And spent more time with those I love
Been more willing to forget the past
And not so quick to judge.

Lord, for the gift of second chances
May I say, "Thank you," from my heart
Teach me to value this gift of life
And make each day a brand new start.

No Guarantees

We buy things with factory rebates
We buy two and get one free
Shop around for things on sale
With a lifetime warranty.

We eat foods that have preservatives
Dress in the original designs
Our boots and coats are weather proof
To stand the test of time.

We send away for coupons
So we can pay a little less
Order books and tapes to help us learn
Quick ways to become a success.

As humans we all try our best
To stay young and fancy free
Try as we might the fact remains
Life has no guarantees!

Cleanliness Is Next To Godliness

Cleanliness is next to Godliness
I once heard a dear friend say
But I'm sure if God meant that for me
He'd add more hours to my day!

Most people have one drawer for junk
At last count I had four
I often have to press real hard
To shut a cupboard door.

I'm full of good intentions
Resolutions, yes quite a few
I'm sure I have a book somewhere
To tell me what to do.

Yes, once again I'll read it
And once again, I'll try
Dear God, could I get organized
Just once before I die?

My Mouth

It runs when it shouldn't
It eats too much food
It often determines
If I'm in a bad mood.

It rules my whole body
And programs my mind
It reacts with a vengeance
Yet, more often it's kind.

If I just had the secret
To the trap of its door
I could pack it and sell it
On the shelves of the stores.

But I have a feeling
Down deep in my soul
It's a constant battle
To keep it under control.

The mouth of the righteous is a well of life.
But violence covers the mouth of the wicked.

Prov. 10 vs. 11-12, New KJV

Love Is Kind

When someone says, "you're beautiful"
And you know you look a mess
When someone says, "you did just great"
And you know you failed the test.

When someone says, "I'm proud of you"
And you've half-way done your job
When someone says, "you're losing weight"
And you feel like such a slob.

When someone says, "you can make it"
And you know you haven't tried
When someone says, "I'm sorry"
And you won't let go of pride.

When someone says, "you're special"
And you feel worthless as a dime
When someone says, "I believe in you"
And you've blown it one more time.

When someone says, "love is gentle"
And you say, "love is blind"
When someone says, "I love who you are"
They're really saying, "love is kind!"

Mood Swings

There are days I feel I'm in control
Of body, spirit, mind and soul
Everything I do is going fine
I'm running with the race of time.

There are days it seems I've lost it all
My dreams have died, I've missed the call
Whatever I say or do or feel
Ends up to be no big deal.

There are days when all the sky seems blue
Nothing is too hard to do
I see the sun and feel the breeze
I sail through life with quite an ease.

There are days I seem to come un-glued
I just can't seem to shake the mood
Nothing in the world seems fair
Whatever comes, I just don't care.

There are days I win no matter what
I seem to laugh and joke a lot
I greet each person with a smile
And try to go that extra mile.

There are days I want to stay in bed
With the covers pulled over my head
I won't go out, let no one in
Like an animal caged inside a pen.

There are days I seem to swing around
I'm up and down and all around
These moods are quite a cross to bear
And I'm left dangling in the air.

Mirror — Mirror

As I look into the mirror
Many faces do I see
There is a girl of three years old
Staring back at me.

Then I see a girl at age of six
With teeth missing when she smiles
Appearing is a teenager
Dressed in crazy styles.

Before me is a woman
Who is married and a mom
She's wandering in confusion
Trying to find where she belongs.

Then all at once I see her
An heir to Christ the King
And the woman in the mirror
Could accomplish anything.

Fire At The Creek Bank

We didn't have any brothers, but we always had the neighbor boys to do things with. On one of our adventures, we decided that we would do a little fishing. At least, the boys would. Gloria and I would do the cooking.

We got an iron skillet and some lard, fishing poles and matches. The first thing we did was try to get the fire started. Gloria swears that mom said, "If you build a fire and keep quiet, the fish will bite." I remember no such conversation.

Upon arriving, we also discovered we had nothing to clean the fish with, but we never made it to that point anyway. Somehow our little fire turned into a bigger one and the flames began to spread quickly over the area. Two older guys happened to be walking down by the dam and saw the fire. One took off his coat and dipped it into the water and began smothering the flames.

I stayed behind with my friend, while Gloria and hers took off running back to the house. Not thinking before talking, she told mom that I was dead and the whole woods were on fire. Poor mom! She called the fire department and was going hysterical.

I was unaware that any of this was going on. I emerged from the woods, only to find firemen and neighbors with a look of shock on their faces. I didn't know that I was supposed to be dead! After mom found out I was all right, she proceeded to remove two switches from a tree and the only thing that was burning was our rear ends.

Our friends went home, the fire trucks headed back to town and neighbors got to witness our welcome from the woods.

To this day, fishing is not one of my hobbies!

The Not So Great Idea

Every day while getting off the bus, my sister, Gloria and I would admire the beautiful gladiolus that lined the driveway of a neighbor. We came up with the brilliant idea that we would pick a big bouquet and take them home to mom. We were still pretty little, so we just picked them off until both of our arms were full. Oh how happy mom would be after she received the lovely gift we had for her. Wrong!

I'll never forget the look of horror on her face when we came strutting in with the flowers. She knew right away where they came from and she didn't hesitate to tell us that they were going back. But she had to take care of us first. Well, you know the rest. I always thought it would have been nice if she would have at least thanked us first.

It was many years later when I experienced the same horror. My daughter, Angie and the neighbor boy, brought me the biggest bouquet of daffodils you ever saw. They proudly told me that they had picked every one just for me. Those daffodils had lined the side of the Methodist church just up the block.

There I was in the same situation my mother had been in years ago. But there was a difference this time. Angie did not get a spanking. I did thank her and put the flowers in a vase. It was hard to have a straight face, and lecture her on taking things from other people's yards that weren't hers.

They say, "what goes around, comes around." This was only one of the memorable occasions I have found it to be true.

Tales Of A Poet

Just sit me by a river bank
Where the water flows so free
With pen in hand I start to write
Of things my eyes can see.

The beauty all around me
Rushes words into my mind
The grass so green beneath my feet
Hold the treasures I must find.

And as each touch of nature
Hosts the fragrances of Spring
I have a chance to talk with God
About oh, so many things.

He talks and as I listen
New poems start to rhyme
My thoughts go then on paper
To be read from time to time.

Inspirational

HOLY BIBLE

c.F. Stark

Good Morning Jesus

Good morning, Jesus, how are you
Leave your shoes on, that's ok,
I haven't scrubbed my kitchen yet
It's on my list of chores today.
I see that snow is still on the ground,
So come in and warm your hands.
I'll pour us a cup of coffee
And we'll talk about our plans.
I've set this chair aside for you
So we can see each other's face.
I like to talk direct to you
And from now on, that's your place.
I've decided today is your turn
To talk of things from A to Z.
I've poured my heart out to you
Now, you pour yours out to me.
You say that you are lonely
And your heart feels hurt today,
That no one ever listens
To the things you have to say?
You say, your days are busy
Filling other people's needs,
That your eyes are sore from crying
You try hard, but can't succeed?
You say you cannot understand
Why we do these things to you,
After all the love you've promised
Do we feel it's all untrue?
Oh Jesus, I'm so sorry
That I've daily passed you by,

I know that I've caused many
Tears to fill your eyes.
I'm so glad you came and talked with me
I want you to know I really care
And my house is always open
When you've got things you need to share.
Friends stop in to see me
And Jesus you come too,
But when you can't come in person
I'll tell you what I'll do.
The chair that's at this table
Will always be for you,
So no matter what time of the day
I'll pretend that you're here too.
You say you must be leaving?
You feel better, I'm so glad,
Because Jesus, you are really
The best friend I've ever had.
Tell the angels I said good morning
I know they're busy too
Keeping everything in Heaven
So beautiful for you.
When I come to live in your house
We'll have coffee every day
Until then, please come and visit
When you've got things you want to say.

— Excerpt from *Daisies and Me*

Does Jesus Hear A Whisper

Does Jesus hear a whisper
When you call upon his name
Does He hear a cry in the midst of night
When our body aches in pain?

Does Jesus hear a whisper
On a cold and rainy day
When a child asks him for sunshine
So they can go outside and play?

Does Jesus hear a whisper
Of thoughts deep within our heart
When all life's daily struggles
Are tearing us apart?

Does Jesus hear a whisper
Of a farmer on his plow
As he prays about the weather
For his crops to grow somehow?

Does Jesus hear a whisper
When a doctor gives up hope
That a parent's child may not survive
The effects of alcohol and dope?

Does Jesus hear a whisper
Of a soldier all alone
When the fear of war is raging
And he longs to be back home?

Does Jesus hear a whisper
Yes, I believe it's true!
He goes by faith and not by sound
To bring joy to me and you.

Give ear to my prayer, O God; and
hide not thyself from my supplication

Psalm 55 vs. 1 KJV

My Favorite Gift

Of all the things I've been given
In my life from time to time
I'd have to say my memory
Is a favorite one of mine.

At any time I can go back
To my earlier childhood days
It's like being in a video
I choose the story that it plays.

I can chat with aunts and uncles
Sit in grandma's rocking chair
Just close my eyes and pick a place
And instantly be there.

I can go to the Rocky Mountains
Walk the shores along Cape Cod
Every day I love to open
This special gift from God!

The memory of the righteous is blessed.

Prov. 10-7 New KJV

My Pumpkins and Celery

It was the fall season and I was talking to God about wanting some pumpkins to decorate around the corn stalks, by my kitchen door. I didn't want to cut out faces in them, I just wanted them as a fall decoration. There were other things more important that I needed, so I didn't really want to spend the money on them, yet I knew they would look so nice by my door. It was just a little conversation between God and I, and I went on about my business cleaning the house.

I was getting a little hungry, and opened the refrigerator to look for a snack. For some reason, I wanted celery and of course that was the one thing I didn't buy when I went to the store. As I closed the fridge, I silently commented, "Lord, I sure wish I would have bought some of that celery." Again, I went back to cleaning.

A couple hours later my parents pulled up in the drive and I went out to meet them. I invited them to come in, but mom said, "No, we're not going to stay honey, your dad and I were out driving around on some back roads and a man had a whole load of pumpkins he was selling. I know how much you like to decorate with them, so take the ones you want." I began to cry, and mom said, "They're only pumpkins, you don't have to cry over them." I said, "Mom, you don't understand, I just told God how much I would like to have some pumpkins!"

It doesn't end there! As she went to close the car door, she said, "Could you use a bunch of celery, the produce stand had three bunches for a dollar?" "I'm going to give you one and give the others to your sisters." Needless to say, I cried again.

Nothing is too little for God to care about. I had the pumpkins and celery to prove it!

Mom's Glasses

Of all the things mom left behind after she died, I wanted her glasses. To some they are just a plastic frame, holding two pieces of glass. Oh, but to me they hold a lifetime of memories.

Many times when I need to make a decision, I will go and pick up her glasses and say, "Okay mom, how do you see this situation, what advice do you have for me?" Even though I can't see out of them, I can see through them! Having her glasses is like having her alive again.

I often just sit and hold them and I find myself in places where we used to go, such as grocery stores. Even if she was wearing those glasses, I still had to read the fine print on the cans and boxes to her. I can still see her writing down the scores when we used to play *Yahtzee*. Then there are the TV shows we used to watch together. My favorite memories are of sitting on the porch and watching all the cars and people go by. In the summer we would drink coffee and eat apples from the tree across the street.

It's still amazing to me, that she never used them to read recipes. She never needed any! But she was the best cook in the world.

I remember the excitement as she would read her birthday, Mother's Day and Christmas cards. I think she saved every card anyone ever gave her. She always used them as she rubbed off her lottery tickets. She had great plans for us kids if she ever won.

Oh how she must have felt, when she had to read the death certificates of five of her children, her two sisters and then her husband. Only to later read her own diagnosis of throat cancer. Her glasses were used to read the time on the clock to take her twenty-six pills a day.

Finally, to lay and look at her family and friends before she died.

Is it possible to see what someone is saying? Because when I look at her glasses, I see her saying, "Oh how I loved you kids, and I hated to leave you, but I was so sick. I just wanted it to be over. Your dad was waiting for me. I went home."

I then see a smile. I am left with the memories.

The Flashlights

A promise is a promise! That was the reassurance we gave our dad before he died.

You see, dad always feared the dark. He never told us why, but mom said that someone had scared him while he was walking through a graveyard one night. I guess he never got over it, because mom was the one who always got up in the middle of the night if we heard strange noises.

Dad was so paranoid about the dark, that he made us promise that when he died, we would put a flashlight at the top and bottom of his casket.

His favorite color was blue, so I found two blue ones. I've always been one for matching colors, no matter what the item may be. Luckily, the funeral director went along with our plans. He also informed us that this was not the strangest request he had ever dealt with.

After the calling hours and funeral services were over, I took the flashlights and placed one by his pillow and the other one at the bottom of his feet. I made sure they were turned on before I let them close the casket. Thus, the promise had been kept!

It might seem crazy, but I really felt that dad knew the lights were on and that he was at peace. It tore at my heart for weeks, wondering how long the batteries would last. I wanted the lights to somehow give him comfort and warmth under that dark, cold ground.

I was going to call the EverReady Company and find out just how long their batteries last, but I didn't think I could deal with the answer.

Just how long will those batteries last? Maybe as long as they stay on in my heart. It's been seven years now, and I haven't decided to turn the lights out yet.

You see, a promise goes on forever.

Give And It
Shall Be Given

I set out for a shopping trip to find myself a little present. Something I felt I deserved for all the aggravation I had been going through. You know how we all get now and then? Well, I collect squirrels, so what better thing to buy myself than an adorable little figurine to look at. I went into the store and it didn't take me long to spot the one I wanted. It just so happened, that this store wrapped for free. So, I decided to have the gift wrapped, since I was giving it to myself. I didn't want to admit this to the clerk, but as she was putting on the paper I had picked out, which by the way also had squirrels on it, I decided to tell her that it was for me. I told her that I had a very rough week, and when I got home I was going to make a cup of coffee, go sit in my rocker and open the gift that I had just bought. We laughed and talked a while, and she began to tell me about one of the ladies in the store who also collected squirrels. Not too many people collect them, so it was a conversation piece.

I spotted another squirrel while I was there and I put it in layaway, just in case I had another rough day! Carrying my beautifully gift wrapped package out to the car, the Lord spoke to my heart, "Give the squirrel to the lady she was talking about." I couldn't believe what I was hearing in my spirit. I said, "Lord, you have got to be kidding, I just bought this, it's wrapped so pretty, and when I get home, I know just where it is going to sit." Ignoring God, I started the car and began driving. I got as far as two stores down, when that inner voice said, "Take the squirrel and give it to that lady." After a few more pleas with God, I opened the door to the store and asked the clerk if the woman she was telling me about was a Christian. She told me that she was. I said, "Good, then she will understand what I mean, when you tell her that God told me to give it to her." The lady said, "But you just bought this for yourself." I replied, "Yes, I know, but God said to give it away, so here it is." She said, "Well, what is your name?" I told her I'd rather not give my name and then I left.

All the way home, I repeatedly told the Lord that I just couldn't understand why of all things I had to give that squirrel away. It was an evening of no coffee, no rocking chair and no gift to open. I just sat looking at the shelf and thought, "I sure hope that lady loves that squirrel as much as I would have."

A day or two later, I got a phone call from the lady who received the squirrel. The first thing I asked her was how in the world she got my name and phone number. She got it from the card I filled out when I laid away the other squirrel. She proceeded to tell me her name and that she had been going through a very rough time in her life. A time of wondering if God even cared about her anymore, and if it was all worth it to even be a Christian. She then told me that I could never imagine what my gift had done to lift her spirits. Somehow, through that gift, she realized that if someone cared enough to obey God to give her something that she loved so much, then she had the faith to believe once again.

Several of the ladies in that store were blessed by that story. I had told my boss about it, and she insisted on giving me the money to buy another one just like it for myself. Everyone got blessed all over again.

Would you believe that very same day my boss gave me the money to go get that squirrel, another girlfriend of mine dropped by the office. She had a package and when handing it to me said, "I don't understand it, I thought I was going shopping for myself, but the Lord told me to get this for you."

It was a beautiful picture of a squirrel that now hangs in my upstairs room above my desk. It just so happened, that before I left for work that morning, I had said, "Lord, I'd love to find a nice picture to hang there, something with the colors to match the wallpaper."

Give it and it shall be given! You'll never know how many times or in how many ways, this has been true in my life.

She Can Talk

The stress of everything and the condition of my mother's health began to take its toll on her. After days in the coronary care unit, we discovered that mom had a stroke. It effected her speech and she could no longer talk.

Days passed and all we could do was try to understand what she wanted. It became very frustrating to her and to all of us. Our relatives came in from out of state to see her, and she could not correspond with them. My mother had always had the gift of gab and this was a very difficult time for her. She knew in her mind what she was saying, but it was not coming through her lips. The doctors had a picture chart for mom and us as a form of communication.

I began to praise God each visit I took to the hospital. I praised him for all the years that she did talk. I also apologized to him for all the complaints I made when I thought she called me too many times a day, or when she gave advice I really didn't want to hear.

For some reason I was able to understand a lot of what she wanted and this was a blessing. Many times when I would go in to see her, she would be in tears, and I would leave in tears. Never had I felt so hopeless about a situation.

Thoughts went through my mind of never being able to talk with mom on the phone again. Oh, the things we take for granted.

The doctor had planned for a speech therapist to come home and work with mom three days a week. During this time, my dad was in critical condition with his cancer. I began to cry out to God and ask him to please heal my mother of this stroke. We needed her; dad needed her. I prayed all the way to the hospital and all the way to her room.

She was coming home that day, and I just didn't know how we were going to handle it all. I walked into her room and mom was sitting up on the bed reading a newspaper. I was totally shocked, because the day before she could not comprehend much of anything. It was apparent that the speech therapist had just left, because there were pictures and instructions on how to care for mom on her little dresser. But something had transpired between the time the doctor had left and I had arrived.

In disbelief, I said to mom "What are you doing?" She replied that she was reading the newspaper to see how the stocks were doing. With tears streaming down my face, I cried, "Mom, you can talk, you can talk!" She looked at me as if to say, "Well, what's the big deal?" I ran out to the nurses's station and told them to come quick, that mom was talking and reading the paper. They literally ran into her room. She just sat looking at us, like nothing had ever happened to her. The nurse on duty told me that she had never seen a stroke patient recover so quickly or fully. Mom was a miracle. Fortunately, most of the ordeal, she could not even remember, but our family would never forget.

My prayers had been answered. Mom could talk. When she called me for the first time on the phone, I can't tell you what a joy it was.

Several years later she was diagnosed with throat cancer. She prayed that God would let her keep her voice until she died. Her prayers were answered. Toward the end, her voice was a little weak, but she got her wish to be able to communicate with her friends and family.

I guess you could say that she was a miracle until her last day here on earth.

My Shiny New Silverware

I was doing my dishes one day, and while I was putting away the silverware, I quietly said to God, "You know, I've had this *Fingerhut* silverware for several years now, and it has held up nicely, but I sure would like to have some new for special occasions. I then began to thank him for my dishes, my kitchen, and just all sorts of things that popped into my mind.

Well, the very next day when I went into work, my boss handed me a little catalog to look at. I said, "What is this?" She replied, "Look through that and pick yourself out a set of silverware. I want you to have a service for twelve." I began to share with her how I had just prayed the night before for some new silverware. Not only did I get that, but a beautiful wooden case to put it in.

Don't ever feel that your prayers are not heard by God. But also, make sure to remember to thank Him for the things you already have.

Every Thanksgiving I try and remember to give my boss a call and thank her for that lovely silverware and for the blessing it was to me.

Christina, You Must Praise Me Too

The doctors had only given my father two more weeks to live. The brain tumor they had tried to remove had grown back twice its size in a matter of fourteen days. He was in so much pain that he was being given morphine every two hours. It was so heartbreaking to watch him suffer like that.

I had began reading some books on Praise. The teachings were that we should learn to praise God in all situations. Not necessarily for them, but in them.

I had spent the night with dad in the hospital because he was feeling so badly. There were several occasions when he would cry out in pain, even after receiving the doses of morphine. It was about two o'clock in the morning and I was sitting there watching him and talking to God. Dad had finally gone to sleep for a while and I was thanking God for that. I also began to tell God that I really didn't understand all that stuff about praise, but I wanted to start doing it. I admitted that it was too hard to give him praise from my heart, but I was willing to speak it from my lips.

Just about the time I finished telling this to God, my dad cried out, "Oh God." My first thought was "Lord, didn't you hear anything I just said to you?" "I was thanking you that dad could finally sleep, now he's hurting again." At the same time, my dad raised one of his arms in the air and then the other.

His eyes were closed, so he was still sleeping. After both arms were raised, he cried out again, "Oh God, I just want to praise you God!"

It was then I knew the Lord spoke to me and said, "Christina, if your father can praise me, you must praise me too."

There were only three people in that room that morning, dad, me, and God. I began to praise God for everything from that day on. That is what got me through all those hospital visits and the sickness.

The best part of all is, my dad got better and lived another ten months.

There is power in praise and it definitely works.

What I want from you is your true thanks;
I want your promises fulfilled.
I want you to trust me in your times of trouble,
so I can rescue you, and you can give me glory.

Psalms 50-vs 14 & 15 (Living Bible)

The Chicken Coop And Stable

The story has been told to me many times over, about how my parents came to the small town of Waynesburg to live. There were no places to rent and my mother was pregnant with me. The only available place was a building that had been used for a chicken coop. They decided to take it!

My mother got orange crates and used them as her cupboards. She bought white paper from the grocery store that they used to wrap meat in, and that became her wallpaper. She used sheets for doorways and partitions between the rooms. With little money and a lot of hard work, she and dad turned that coop into their palace.

I, Christina Faye Brown, was born there. Mom and dad were always so thankful for what they had.

One day I was feeling sorry for myself. I felt like there were so many things I wanted to do, but life hadn't dealt me the right cards. It was then, that a still small voice inside me said, "I was born in a stable and I turned out fine." I knew that it was Jesus speaking to me.

Yes, He was born in a stable and they lay Him in a manger. I was born in a chicken coop and slept in an orange crate. The moral of this story is: it doesn't matter where your life begins, what matters is what you do with it after you grow up.

My Final Visit

On the eve of her death, mom was sleeping and I kept shaking her to wake her up. She opened her eyes and said, "Why do you feel it necessary to keep waking me up?" I told her it was because I wanted to hear her talk to me. She informed me that she would rather sleep than talk.

How I longed to hear one of her childhood stories just one more time. We used to tease her about repeating so many things. That day, it would have been a welcome sound, but she was too weak to speak. Even the little bell she used to ring when she needed us, lay hushed on the stand by her bed. Its clamor would have meant life and hope. Its silence told our fate.

On the morning of her final day, the Hospice nurse arrived and took mom's vital signs. Her eyes were full of sympathy as she told us it would only be a matter of hours. At our request, she left us alone with mom and we promised to call when it was over.

I was the only one who didn't get to be with dad the day he died. What a blessing it was to be there with my mom. Morning lingered into afternoon and we decided that my sisters would go home for a while and I would call them when the time grew near. I took the opportunity to crawl into bed with mom. It was comforting to me as well as her, as I stroked her hair and let her know how much we loved and would miss her. We had been told that the hearing is the last of the senses to go, so I wanted to make sure she heard only loving things. She had taught me a song when I was three years old called, "Known Only To Him", and I sang that to her, along with several of her other favorites.

Tears of sadness rolled down my face as I recalled the statement from the Hospice nurse. She said, "It's important to remember when you become a caretaker that you become the parent and they are the child." The roles had truly reversed. I was comforting my mother as she once did me with her singing.

The gurgling sound in her throat was my signal to call my sisters. But first, I went to the back porch and looked up to Heaven with a plea from my heart, to please not let mom strangle to death in her own fluid.

As I rushed back into the room, there was a pitiful gaze in her eyes. I couldn't tell if it was a look of fear, that I had left, or she knew she was dying and couldn't speak. I'll go to my grave wondering what story she was telling with her eyes.

I sat on her bed and took her hand. With a broken heart, I said, "Mom, I'm here, I didn't leave." There was no time to make a phone call as I said my final words; "It's alright mom, you put up a good fight. Just go home and be with Jesus. Dad is waiting for you and we love you."

There was one short gasp for air and it was over. April 6th, 1992 was my final visit with mom. In a split second, I knew what it was like to be an orphan.

Still Holding On

Hands have always intrigued me, but there is one pair of hands that are very special to me, and they belong to my husband, Dean.

His hands joined in mine during ball games, picnics, and school dances. They placed a ring upon my finger twenty-seven years ago, as he made a promise to always be mine. They embraced our daughter when she was born and have been used to support our family over the years.

They have tenderly held me when I was sick and carried me all the little extras to make me feel better.

He is a carpenter and I just marvel at the things his hands have made. Many houses have become homes because of his talents with wood.

Although, just like in all marriages, we thought of throwing in the towel now and then, but I'm so glad we are still *holding on*.

There are times while he is sleeping, that I look at his hands and thank God that I was blessed to be the woman he placed in their care.

This Is Only A Test

I can't think of any Bible character who went through more trying times than Job. His faith was daily being tested.

There have been many times in my life, when I felt like I was never going to get out of God's classroom. The tests of life were more than I cared to deal with or study and prepare myself for. In our regular classrooms, the teacher usually announced when there would be a test. But God is different. He chooses to give "surprise exams."

He also has a unique grading system. There are no F's for failure. You are allowed to take the test over as many times as it takes to learn the lesson. If we are willing to let Him train us mentally, physically and spiritually, the tests become easier and easier.

So, if you are going through things in your life, and you feel like closing the books and giving up, remember "this is only a test!"

God is allowing you to go from kindergarten to grade school, to high school and then off to college. Hang in there! The *Master's* Degree is well worth waiting for!

Who's The Boss

Many times we ask God for His help and then we try to tell Him how to do everything. We don't want to wait and put our trust in His timing, but we want it NOW!

Why do you suppose it is so hard to let go and let God? It's because we want to be our own boss. Think about it. In the natural life, when we go to our boss with a problem we stay out of it. We feel that it's their job to handle whatever comes up. Why are we so different when it comes to our spiritual life?

When we work on the job, we know that we don't get paid for that work until payday. But if we do something for God, we expect immediate rewards.

I think it's time to put things in perspective and realize that if it wasn't for our Heavenly boss, we would have no earthly boss. And since we don't go in the office or place of work and tell them what to do, we need to quit trying to tell God what to do.

The next time we get up to do a day of *spiritual* work, let's go about it with a new attitude. Let God be the boss! He should decide what our pay is and if we get a bonus or vacation time. In my walk with Him, I have found that He gives a lot of unexpected raises!

Give Me A J-E-S-U-S

It always amazes me how people can go to ball games and yell and scream, but when anyone makes a noise in church, it's a big deal.

Have any of those ball players ever provided your needs? Ever healed a loved one? Ever made a way where there was no way? Do they even know your name? Do they know how may stars are in the sky and know all their names?

No, and after you leave that game, you can guarantee they won't ever know you had been there.

Why not start cheering the one who holds you in the palm of His hand? Why not cheer the one who never quits when the game gets tough? God has scored more points than any player and He desires to make you a winner!

The next time you go to your church and find people worshipping the Lord, why not join in yourself?

Let Him know that you believe in Him and appreciate everything He does to make your life worth living.

Jesus needs a lot more cheerleaders in this game of life!

I Ain't Foolin' With It

"I ain't foolin' with it"
Would make an English teacher cry
But inside this tiny sentence
Many dreams begin to die.

"I ain't foolin' with it"
Relays a message from the heart
Because what you're really saying
Is you quit before you start.

"I ain't foolin' with it"
Could destroy the souls of men
When said in words of anger
Sew beginnings to an end.

"I ain't foolin' with it"
Must be followed by a prayer
"Dear God, somehow in all this mess
Please show me, you're still there!"

Circle Of Love

Mom used to dress us all alike, as though we were triplets. There are many ways we act just like each other yet today. I have always loved my two sisters, Gloria and Rose, but there is one occasion that stands out in my mind.

That was the day we had to divide mom and dad's estate. It was then, we all stood in a circle and prayed for wisdom to evenly and fairly distribute everything.

There we stood with broken hearts, yet willing to lovingly let each other have what meant the most to them. There was peace in that house until every last thing was taken. One minute we were crying, and the next laughing over all they had accumulated.

I wish every family that loses a loved one could get along like we did. The Bible says, "Jesus is a friend who sticks closer than a brother." I truly believe that we three sisters had a brother watching over us. You see, we invited Him into that circle, and He took what could have been a disaster and turned it into one of the best days of our lives.

He will do the same for you! All He needs is an invitation.

He's Some Kind of King

We had taken dad's favorite picture of Jesus and hung it on the wall of his hospital room. The brain tumor had taken away most of his memory, and we couldn't bear the thought of him forgetting who Jesus was.

Each day, I would ask dad if he knew who was in the picture. On one occasion, he said, "He's my best friend, He never takes his eyes off me." Another day, dad called Him his foreman, because He looked like someone who took charge of everything and was "as smart as a tack." But the best description of all, was the day he said, "He's some kind of King!" His only explanation was, that he "just knew it."

The Bible says, in Matthew 12:34 - "For out of the abundance of the heart, the mouth speaks." How true! The enemy can do all kinds of things to try and destroy our minds and bodies, but thanks be to God, what is hidden in our hearts will remain forever.

You see, my dad's brain did not allow him to remember the name of Jesus, but his heart knew Him perfectly. He described Him as a best friend, someone who is all-knowing and most of all, "Some kind of King!"

Gifts of Love

It's not easy in this fast-paced society, to give "gifts of love." They require time and effort on the part of the giver. Yet, they are treasured forever in the heart of the receiver.

There are many things in our homes that are collecting dust, that we received from those who love us. Even if we lost all of them, we would still be able to hold onto our "gifts of love."

How can this be? Because they are etched in our memory. Such as, my neighbor Arlene, who took care of me every day for three months while I recuperated from an accident. Or Cheri, who took so much time in doing the art work for this book. All these things could never be bought, for a price they are really worth.

Ask God to help you, to wrap yourself up for someone! Everybody needs a "gift of love."

Things

Things is a six letter word that can literally change the course of our lives.

We all get up in the morning with *things* to do. Our goals can't be reached, because we keep letting *things* get in our way. Many lives are in turmoil, because they can't get over all the *things* others have done to them. Divorce rates are high, because they can't agree on *things* in their marriage. People delay serving the Lord, because they want to get rid of a few *things* in their life, before they make any commitments. We don't have time for one another, because we have too many *things* going on.

Things are whatever exist in our lives. What *things* are you allowing to rob you of your joy?

Well, now that I have given you a few *things* to think about, let me leave you with this verse:

> *I can do all **things** through Christ*
> *who strengthens me.*

Phillipians 4-13 KJV

Heavenly Dispatch

For years I have been a dispatcher for a trucking company. Little did I realize that God would someday use my job title as an idea for a radio ministry.

When I was young, I used to sing on the radio with my dad and uncle. It always seemed fascinating, knowing your voice was going out over the airways.

One day, I felt God dealing with me to start a radio program. For those of you who don't know what this means, it's when you feel something so strong that it just won't go away. Then you just know it's God! It was not something I took lightly. I spent a year in prayer before I made the final decision. Doors began to open and God and I walked through.

Since I dispatch trucks, I decided to use the title "Heavenly Dispatch." Talking has never been a problem for me, but limiting myself to fifteen minutes has been a real challenge.

Now, I dispatch trucks all week and dispatch the good new of Jesus Christ on Sundays. It has been a very rewarding experience. I count it a privilege to share God's love with the listening audience.

In Closing

Well I have opened the door and let you come in
You have just read my heart from beginning to end
Each page tells a story of the life I have lived
What more can I say? What more can I give?

I hope it has helped you to feel better inside
To laugh and to cry and to swallow your pride
I pray you will be thankful for the big and the small
Knowing that God is the giver of all.

My flesh and my heart faileth;
but God is the strength of my heart,
and my portion forever.

Psalm 73-26 (KJV)

Order Form

Please rush me the following book:

Title	Price	Qty	Amount
I Give You My Heart	9.95	___	_____

Ohio Sales Tax _____
(6%, Ohio Residents Only)
*Shipping _____

Grand Total _____

* Shipping: $2.50 for 1st book; 1.00 each additional book.

Name _____

Address _____

City/State/Zip _____

Phone _____

Please mail order and make checks payable to:

Christina Stark
P.O. Box 15
East Sparta, Ohio 44626

If you would like to have Christina be a guest speaker or singer, please contact her at the above address.